The Christian's
Conflict Handbook
on Resolution

The Christian's Conflict Handbook on Resolution

BIBLICAL PRINCIPLES FOR RESTORING AND PREVENTING BROKEN RELATIONSHIPS

"FOR WE DO NOT WRESTLE AGAINST FLESH AND BLOOD. . . ."
EPHESIANS 6:12

Greg M. Sumii

PROVIDENCE HOUSE PUBLISHERS
Franklin, Tennessee

Copyright 1998 by California Southern Baptist Convention

All rights reserved. Written permission must be secured from the publisher
to use or reproduce any part of this book, except for brief quotations in
critical reviews or articles.

Permission is granted to reproduce any of the student worksheets.

Scripture taken from the New American Standard Bible, © 1960, 1962, 1963, 1968,
1971, 1972, 1973, 1975, 1977 by The Lockman Foundation. Used by persmission.

Printed in the United States of America

02   01   00   99   98   1   2   3   4   5

Library of Congress Catalog Card Number: 98-65878

ISBN: 1-57736-098-2

Cover design by Gary Bozeman

PROVIDENCE HOUSE PUBLISHERS
238 Seaboard Lane • Franklin, Tennessee 37067
800-321-5692

TO MY WIFE
YOLANDA
AND CHILDREN
GREG JR. AND FELICIA
FOR THEIR UNWAVERING SUPPORT
OF MY MINISTRY.

Contents

FOREWORD

OCCASIONALLY MATERIAL WILL CROSS MY DESK WHICH HAS UNUSUAL BENEFIT both to the reader and the leader of such material. THE CHRISTIAN'S HANDBOOK ON CONFLICT RESOLUTION by Greg M. Sumii is just such material. It is biblically sound, psychologically worthy of good counseling techniques, and possesses sound teaching and training principles. The use of this material meets a serious need to apply these areas in conflict resolution both for pastor, the church, and church members. The application of these resolution principles will assist families, friends, and Christians in general to discover that hurtful relationships have no place in the Christian's vocabulary, much less actions.

Greg Sumii's spiritual approach, strengthened by biblical application to the problems people have with each other, is most refreshing. A serious study and application of the material in this book will assist the pastor, the church, and family members to not only preclude conflict, but resolve conflict that may have begun.

In a time when pastors and churches have major conflict, where families are torn apart with divorce, and where friendships are ripped asunder, viable material which approaches these situations with intent on resolution, and a renewal of Christian responsibilities to each other, THE CHRISTIAN'S HANDBOOK ON CONFLICT RESOLUTION will be most helpful. In fact, it should be the major textbook for seminary training for pastors and church leaders dealing with pastoral ministry and counseling. I commend this book for times like these dealing with conflict resolution!

C. B. Hogue, Executive Director Emeritus
California Southern Baptist Convention

PREFACE

BIBLICAL CONFLICT RESOLUTION PRINCIPLES SHOULD BE TAUGHT IN BASIC discipleship for every Christian. The church has faltered here and the lack of training has had devastating consequences. The divorce rate of Christian couples is now about the same as those who are not Christians (Religious News Service, Feb. 11, 1997). Christians are fighting at church. In many churches, the leaders are not unified and are in conflict. Forced termination of pastors is a major problem. So many Christians are wounded today because of the hurtful actions of other Christians. Conflicts are at a crisis level.

As a family counselor and conflict mediator for churches, I am constantly reminded that all Christians need training on conflict resolution. Many have tried to resolve their disagreements, only to end up more disagreeable! The goal of Biblical conflict resolution is reconciliation in a God-honoring process. God is waiting to bless His resolution principles.

This handbook is formatted to be readily used to provide this training. Each chapter has a leader's section that can serve as a teaching guide. The appendix includes the worksheets for students. The material can also be very valuable for individual study.

For the honor and glory of God, may Christian families and churches resolve to reflect the unfailing love of God. "A new commandment I give to you, that you love one another, even as I have loved you, that you also love one another. By this know all men will know that you are My disciples, if you have love for one another" (John 13:34–35).

INTRODUCTION

RECENTLY TAUGHT A SEMINAR AT GLORIETTA, NEW MEXICO. THE SEMINAR was entitled, "Healing Broken Relationships in a Baptist Church." I mentioned that the title was an oxymoron. Those words should not go together!

What in the world is going on out there? Our testimony is that "Christ in us" makes a radical difference in Christian relationships. To the church's embarrassment and shame, far too many Christian families are breaking down and Christian marriages are ending in divorce. The fabric of many Christian homes is unraveling.

Another growing problem is divisiveness within the church. Unresolved conflicts are tearing up the fellowship of Christ and causing broken relationships in the church. Many churches are firing their pastor and churches continue to splinter. Church members are leaving with open wounds and bitter spirits.

Shouldn't we have a higher standard for the behavior of God's people? The Bible clearly teaches that when we became Christians, we were indwelt by the Holy Spirit, and became new persons in Christ.

The Holy Spirit manifests Himself through the fruit of the Spirit, "love, joy, peace, patience, kindness, goodness, gentleness, faithfulness and self-control" (Gal. 5:22–23). Christ, through the Holy Spirit indwelling us, gives us both the desire and empowerment to relate with Christlike characteristics.

It is an affront to the Holy and Loving God, that Christians are acting to the contrary, saying and doing things that hurt people and damage relationships. For far too long, the churches have allowed sinful behaviors that destroy relationships and hinder the witness of the love of God. Unresolved conflicts and broken relationships are usually ignored or dismissed.

I've heard it said about divorcing, "I thought I had a great deal, it became an ordeal, and now I want a new deal." This thinking and acting is so contrary to the central message of the Bible—RECONCILIATION. Men are to be reconciled with God, and with each other.

Jesus even taught that the two greatest commandments called for right relationships with God and others.

"You shall love the Lord your God with all your heart, and with all your soul, and with all your mind." This is the foremost commandment. And a second is like it, "You shall love your neighbor as yourself." On these two commandments depend the whole Law and the prophets. (Matt. 22:37–40)

What is at stake here? I believe that revival in America may be withheld because of active sin among believers. Gossip, slander, outbursts of anger, maliciousness, unforgiveness, contentiousness and the unwillingness to cooperate toward reconciliation are literally destroying relationships. These behaviors are of the dark world and dishonor our God of light and love.

I believe that relational abuse among Christians could be hindering the sending of spiritual renewal to the Christian home and church. Not only have countless people been hurt, but the witness of Christ has been disgraced. The blood is on the hands of Christians!

God has already promised to send revival.

And My people who are called by my name humble themselves and pray, and seek My face and turn from their wicked ways, then I will hear from heaven, will forgive their sin, and heal the land. (2 Chron. 7:14)

The promise hinges on the condition that believers repent of their sins. Individual repentance must happen for the sinful behavior among Christians in their relationships. Corporate repentance is warranted for the toleration of hurtful or sinful behavior within the church.

This handbook on biblical conflict resolution is intended to equip Christians to maintain the Lordship of Christ in all relationships and fellowships. Healthy and biblical conflict resolution principles should be taught in basic Christian discipleship. I am amazed at how many Christians just simply don't know what to do to resolve conflict, especially in a way that honors and glorifies God. The Word of God is filled with clear teachings on how to resolve conflict and restore unity. The material in this book is designed to be readily used in individual or group Bible study.

In 2 Corinthians 5:18–20, the apostle Paul teaches that we are to be ministers of reconciliation. This is our God-assigned mission in life. My prayer is that unity and reconciliation in relationships will become our trademark, for God's honor and glory. Christians must lay down their arms against each other, and join together in the fight against the true enemy, the devil. "For we do not wrestle against flesh and blood. . . ."

UNIT I

RESOLVING CONFLICTS
IN RELATIONSHIPS

CHAPTER 1

Relational Conflict and Emotional/Spiritual Warfare

For our struggle is not against flesh and blood, but against the rulers, against the powers, against the world forces of this darkness, against the spiritual forces of wickedness in the heavenly places. (Eph. 6:12)

I HAVE PERFORMED MANY WEDDING CEREMONIES. INVARIABLY, THE BRIDE and groom promise to love, honor and respect each other forever, with glitter in their eyes! Nothing can get in their way . . . except maybe a little conflict. The conflict might be caused by hurtful words in an argument. Remember the saying as a child, "Sticks and stones may break my bones but words will never hurt me." Guess what? That is not true. Hurtful words penetrate deep and wound the spirit. Somehow the luster quality of the relationship fades.

Open communication can become a battlefield. There is attacking and defending. A certain toleration level is attained and the relationship reduces to protecting oneself from being hurt by the spouse. The fantastic spouse that was such a blessing is now more like a curse. Thoughts begin to surface, "I don't need this," or, "I want out."

That dear love of your life gradually becomes an adversary. It is natural to fight or flee from an enemy. Divorce and the freedom from this enemy become the logical solution. The Bible teaches that this is NOT the solution. As a matter of fact, the other person is not the enemy. The true enemy is the devil.

> Put on the full armor of God, that you may be able to stand firm against the schemes of the devil. For our struggle is not against flesh and blood. . . . (Eph. 6:11–12)

The devil is engaged in an all-out campaign to steal the joy and happiness in the Christian's love relationships. He wants to get us where it really counts!

Here is a diagram explanation of how the devil influences hurtful dynamics between two people. There is the offender who is a difficult, hurtful or mean-spirited person. The offended one is a victim and becomes irritated, hurt, or even devastated. The victim is in a wounded condition and very vulnerable to the devil's temptations to retaliate. The temptations are gossip, slander, threats or retaliation and they look like real good options to the wounded victim.

If the offended party falls for the temptation to retaliate, then the victim can become a victimizer. The original offender may retaliate in return, and a conflicted relationship is perpetuated.

Since the devil is actively involved and sins are committed, these negative encounters need to be reframed as spiritual conflicts (Eph. 6:11–12). The devil preys upon wounded

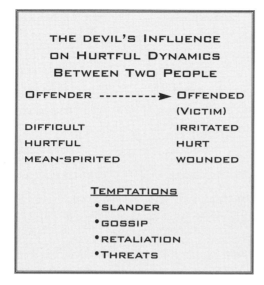

Christians because they are easy and vulnerable targets, while they nurse their wounds.

Satan's nature is depicted in the Bible by the descriptive meaning of his names. By learning his various names, it will be easy to detect when he is scheming or attacking. He is referred to as a tempter, deceiver, accuser, murderer, liar, destroyer, confuser, oppressor, and thief. Have you seen his tracks in your church or love relationship?

The devil's mission field is the church or Christians. His goal is to discredit the witness of the church and hinder God's glory. His strategy is to stir up conflict which will lead to strained or broken relationships. It would greatly please the devil to hurt, weaken or destroy from within the Christian home and church.

At this point, it is a shameful scenario in so many churches and love relationships. Tension builds, anger rages within, leading to open conflicts, then communication shuts down, and relationships are severed.

A Spiritual-Emotive Understanding of Relational Difficulties

The spiritual-emotive perspective on problematic relationships recognizes the inner workings of both spiritual and emotional forces. It is spiritual/emotional warfare. The emotional forces are empowered when negative emotions are left unresolved. There are strong biblical warnings against the harboring of negative emotions.

> Be angry, and yet do not sin; never let the sun go down on your anger, and do not give the devil an opportunity . . . Let all bitterness and wrath and anger and clamor and slander be put away from you, along with all malice. (Eph. 4:26–27, 31)

> See to it that no one comes short of the grace of God; that no root of bitterness springing up causes trouble, and by it many be defiled. (Heb. 12:15)

There are also biblical injunctions about spiritual warfare in relational problems.

> For our struggle is not against flesh and blood, but against the rulers, against the powers, against the world forces of this darkness, against the spiritual forces of wickedness in the heavenly places. (Eph. 6:12)

> Be of sober spirit, be on the alert. Your adversary, the devil, prowls around like a roaring lion, seeking someone to devour. (1 Peter 5:8)

The biblical warnings are so serious that the Holy Spirit grieves when the devil wins control in a Christian's relationships: "And do not grieve the Holy Spirit of God . . ."

(Eph. 4:30). The context of this verse relates to Christians who are hurtful with their actions and words.

The spiritual-emotive approach to resolving conflicts requires two focuses for complete resolution. There must be humble obedience to God, first, removing the negative emotions and second, resisting of the devil to stop his activity from disturbing relationships. "Submit therefore to God. Resist the devil and he will flee from you" (James 4:7).

Case Study

On one occasion, I was very offended by my daughter's actions. I was angry, and I scolded her sternly. She responded with self-defense and anger. The disciplinary discussion escalated and I was consumed with anger. All the while, I was feeling guilty because I teach conferences often about controlling negative emotions. I was definitely out of control and anger was driving me to want to say things in harsh ways that were hurtful to my daughter. I was also fearful that she might become a rebellious teenager.

She continued to resist me, so I made a power move, and sent her to her room. She gladly left me in a hurry and you guessed it . . . slammed her door. We were both out of control. I was feeling so bad and was mad that the devil was gaining the victory in seeing our relationship damaged. I confessed my sin of quarreling with anger and resentment. I resolved to bring peace to our relationship, with God's help. I prayed for God's intervention through me (Phil. 4:13).

I went to her room and humbled myself. I explained that at that moment it didn't matter who was right or wrong. What did matter was that we must love each other. I told her those healing words, "I love you." She responded immediately with the same. We hugged and prayed and thanked God for His love. "Above all, keep fervent in your love for one another, because love covers a multitude of sins" (1 Peter 4:8).

Our anger was replaced with love. The devil left our presence because he can't stand for God to get the glory, and for God's people to be happy!

Unhealthy and hurtful relating violates basic Scriptural injunctions to have Christlike character in the resolving of conflicts. Thus, relational problems are spiritual problems, necessitating a spiritual remedy. The victory is only through Christ. "But in all these things we overwhelmingly conquer through Him who loved us" (Rom. 8:37).

Broken relationships can only be completely restored through Christ and His grace. Forgiveness and love are necessary to bring healing. The Bible teaches that it is the very love and forgiveness received from Christ that we must extend to the other.

> And so, as those who have been chosen of God, holy and beloved, put on a heart of compassion, kindness, humility, gentleness, and patience; bearing with one another, and forgiving each other, whoever has a complaint against any one, just as the Lord forgave you, so also should you. And beyond all these things put on love, which is the perfect bond of unity. And let the peace of Christ rule in your hearts. (Col. 3:12–15a)

LEADER'S SECTION

Teacher's Worksheet

Negative encounters in love relationships need to be reframed as spiritual conflicts (Eph. 5:22–6:9; 6:11–12, 16). The devil schemes to cause difficulty in Christian relationships. The devil preys upon Christians who are wounded emotionally because they are vulnerable targets.

I. Identify the True Enemy
  1. Satan's nature:
    Matthew 4:3 *tempter*
    Revelation 12:10 *deceiver*
    Revelation 12:9 *accuser*
    John 8:44b *liar*
    1 Peter 5:8 *destroyer*
    1 Corinthians 14:33 *confuser*
    Acts 10:38 *oppressor*
    John 10:10a *thief*

  Satan's nature is depicted in the Bible by the descriptive meaning of his names. By learning his various names, it will be easy to detect when he is scheming or attacking.
  2. Satan's mission field: church and individual Christians
  3. Satan's strategy: tempt Christians to be hurtful when out of control emotionally
  4. Satan's goal: destroy the witness of God's love and power in the church and Christian's relationships

II. Consult With the Book of Life
What is a Christian instructed to do when someone is irritating, offensive or hurtful?
  Ephesians 4:15 *speak the truth in love*
  2 Timothy 2:25 *correct with gentleness*
  Matthew 18:15 *confront privately*
  Matthew 5:23–24 *seek reconciliation*
  Matthew 5:44 *show love and pray for them*
  Romans 12:14,21 *examine what you can change in your reactions*
  Colossians 3:13 *bear with them and forgive*
  Colossians 3:23–24 *do it for Christ when you can't sincerely do it for the other*
  1 Peter 2:21–23 *entrust yourself to God, the perfect and righteous Judge*
  Ephesians 4:31 *put aside your negative feelings*
  1 Kings 12:7 *be a servant*

III. Engage In Spiritual Warfare
  1. 2 Corinthians 10:3–5 The weapons of our warfare are *divinely powerful for defeating the devil's strongholds.*
  2. Ephesians 2:6; Revelation 4:2 Take your *position of spiritual authority alongside the throne of Sovereign God.*
  3. Ephesians 6:11–17 Put on the *armor of God and resist the devil.*
  4. Ephesians 6:17–18; Matthew 4:1–11 Command Satan with the authority of *God's Word.*
  5. Romans 8:31, 37 Claim the *victory through Jesus!*
  6. Psalms 18:1–3 Praise God for spiritual victory. He is our *deliverer.*

★See Appendix A, Student Worksheet

CHAPTER 2

ANGER: MANAGE IT OR IT WILL MANAGE YOU

Be angry, and yet do not sin; do not let the sun go down on your anger, and do not give the devil an opportunity. (Eph. 4:26–27)

AFTER SERVING MANY YEARS AS A FAMILY COUNSELOR AND A CHURCH conflict mediator, I have observed Christians behaving in ways that are so harmful. They struggled with control of their attitudes and behavior toward each other. Relationships were damaged and severed.

I personally know numerous Christian couples who were inseparably in love. Then years later, they are literal enemies, full of bitterness and divorced. What happened in those years of relating that led to the deterioration of their love relationship?

I have been called upon by numerous churches to intervene and assist with resolving severe internal conflict. It has been a grievous experience to see God's people hurting, angry, hostile and intolerant of each other. Countless members have left these conflicted churches in utter disdain, appalled at the hurtful behavior within the membership. In some situations, the emotions had escalated out of control, whereby members feared for their own safety! What is going on?

There is a serious problem with very poor self-management. Words and actions are recklessly hurting and damaging relationships among Christians. I get perplexed and scratch my head thinking, "There is something wrong with this picture."

Christians are suppose to be different. Believers were first called "Christians," in Acts 11:26, mainly because they were acting and relating just like Christ. The word Christian means "little Christs" or "Christ in miniature."

Christ and His unconditional love are our standards for conduct and character.

A new commandment I give to you, that you love one another, even as I have loved you, that you also love one another. By this all men will know that you are my disciples, if you have love one for another. (John 13:34–35)

But many Christians are acting like the devil instead of like Christ. Many are angry, bitter, hostile and unforgiving. There is gossiping, backbiting, yelling, name calling, sabotaging, and unfortunately, the list of ungodly behavior goes on and on.

I have come to the conclusion that the problem is basically spiritual. When Christians are fighting, they aren't even aware that there is a spiritual battle between God and the devil for the control of their lives. And there is power from each to be empowered to either act unrighteously or righteously.

Since the nature of the conflict is spiritual, then we can always assume that the Bible has spiritual counsel for resolution. In regards to controlling anger and self, the Bible says in James 1:19–20,

> But let every one be quick to hear, slow to speak and slow to anger, for the anger of man does not achieve the righteousness of God.

Controlling one's anger is absolutely critical for righteousness sake and to preserve relationships. Consider the diagram on p. 9 and Appendix B.

———————

Following the diagram: The offender is offensive with words or actions. It is the offender's responsibility before God to repent. It is the offended person's responsibility to forgive.

Each has their own responsibility to God for the proper response. The reaction of the victim is key, especially if the offender is unrepentant. The victim's reaction will determine if the relationship will be severed. Anger management is crucial.

I believe that it is the victim's poor management of anger that propels the relationship into deterioration. The victim has the power to prevent the relationship from severing, by getting rid of the anger. But, without immediate anger resolution, the victim will naturally not want to forgive and the relationship becomes distant or broken.

Forgiveness means to pardon. It means to pardon even when the other party is undeserving. We must remember that God forgave us when we were so undeserving also. Sometimes, the offending party is either unavailable or unwilling to cooperate. It is not necessary to have the other's cooperation in order to forgive. Often times, the offender has died or has moved away.

Since forgiveness is pardoning, it lets the person off the hook. In the process of letting the other person off the hook, you get yourself off their hook and free from the associated pain of the past. It is the offended who is suffering with bitterness and pain, which can only be healed through forgiveness.

When one is unwilling to forgive, the offender may not even be affected by it. The offended may suffer for a long time without healing, until the decision is made to forgive.

God commands that we forgive. Therefore, true peace is not forthcoming from the Lord until we obey Him and forgive.

The pivotal point is what the victim does with the anger. In Ephesians 4:26–27, the Bible teaches that we are not to harbor anger for very long. When the victim lives with unresolved anger, the Bible warns that the devil will gain a foothold. The devil recognizes that an angry Christian is very impressionable. The devil seeks to influence the Christian to think hateful thoughts and take revengeful actions to hurt in return.

 This is why God says to put away the anger swiftly (Eph. 4:27, 31). Anger can be replaced with sadness and disappointment over the situation and the status of the relationship. Jesus is well acquainted with sadness and grief. In Isaiah 53:3–5, we find that Jesus was despised and forsaken, and bore our sorrows and grief. Jesus knows what it is like to be rejected. In John 1:11, it says, "He came to His own and His own received Him not."

Coming to God in sadness invites the life of God and His inner healing to enter through the Holy Spirit. Psalm 46:1 says, "God is our refuge and strength, a very present help in time of need."

It is devastating to self and the relationship if the anger is not put away. The influence of the devil strengthens from a foothold to a stronghold. The negative emotions begin to control the Christian. The unresolved anger will develop into resentment. In the pool of resentment inside, there is also arrogance and the unwillingness to forgive. The Bible says in James 4:6, "God resists the proud, but gives grace to the humble." The power to forgive, the grace to be free of the bondage, and the grace for healing is forfeited. But a humble Christian is entitled to this grace.

It is at this point that the Christian may be without the watchful care and protection of God. And Satan is like a vulture, snatching his prey without the protection of God. The resentment deepens into bitterness. The Bible warns Christians that bitterness will lead to defilement.

> See to it that no one comes short of the grace of God; that no root of bitterness springing up causes trouble, and by it many are defiled. (Heb. 12:15)

It is when the Christian is defiled that vile evil surfaces from sin nature. The Christian is out of control and the devil has a stronghold.

Things are said and done that are destructive and so regrettable. Ephesians 4:28–29, 31, warns against retaliation, which eventually damages or destroys relationships, and grieves the Holy Spirit.

At this point, the Christian feels totally self-defeated and miserable. It is a condition that is the fulfillment of a warning from Matthew 18:34–35, that the cost or consequence for unforgiveness is a state of inner torment and woundedness.

When I have counseled with bitter persons and the bitterness is given up, invariably underneath, there are buried hurts that surface. That brings us back to the beginning of this cycle.

There could be no healing of the wound, because the hurt is buried alive. The anger and bitterness cover and insulate the pain of the hurt. Therefore, it is critical to move from the initial anger and hurt to sadness, which invites in the life of God for relief and healing. God gives the grace or power to forgive. James 4:6 teaches, "God gives grace to the humble." Finally, there is inner peace and freedom from hurtful negative emotions (John 14:27).

LEADER'S SECTION

Teacher's Chart

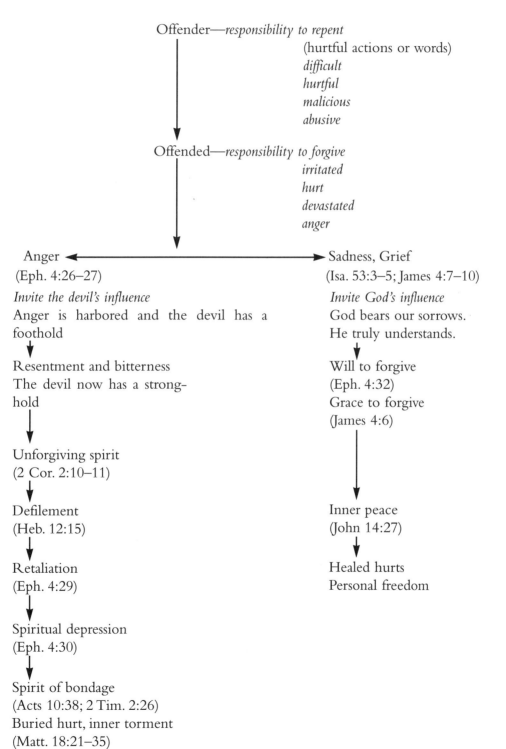

Offender—*responsibility to repent*
(hurtful actions or words)
difficult
hurtful
malicious
abusive

Offended—*responsibility to forgive*
irritated
hurt
devastated
anger

Anger ←——————————————————→ Sadness, Grief
(Eph. 4:26–27)　　　　　　　　　　　　　(Isa. 53:3–5; James 4:7–10)

Invite the devil's influence　　　　　　　*Invite God's influence*
Anger is harbored and the devil has a　　　God bears our sorrows.
foothold　　　　　　　　　　　　　　　He truly understands.

Resentment and bitterness　　　　　　　Will to forgive
The devil now has a strong-　　　　　　(Eph. 4:32)
hold　　　　　　　　　　　　　　　　Grace to forgive
　　　　　　　　　　　　　　　　　　(James 4:6)

Unforgiving spirit
(2 Cor. 2:10–11)

Defilement　　　　　　　　　　　　　Inner peace
(Heb. 12:15)　　　　　　　　　　　　(John 14:27)

Retaliation　　　　　　　　　　　　　Healed hurts
(Eph. 4:29)　　　　　　　　　　　　　Personal freedom

Spiritual depression
(Eph. 4:30)

Spirit of bondage
(Acts 10:38; 2 Tim. 2:26)
Buried hurt, inner torment
(Matt. 18:21–35)

★See Appendix B, Student Worksheet

CHAPTER 3

HEALING HURTS AND RELEASING GOD'S LOVE

*Beloved, let us love one another, for love is from God; and every one
who loves is born of God and knows God. (1 John 4:7)*

AS A MARRIAGE COUNSELOR, I HAVE HEARD A STATEMENT REPEATEDLY THAT
I have to correct. After a spouse has been deeply hurt, especially for a
prolonged period, it is said, "I don't love him/her anymore." My response
is that the feeling of love is buried underneath anger and hurt. You cannot feel negative
and positive feelings at the same time. What is critically important is to take responsibility for the feelings being experienced. To feel anger and hurt beyond the initial
situational response is the choice to harbor those negative feelings. At the same time, it
is a choice to withhold love.

If you are a Christian, the love is still there! The Bible teaches that God is love. "The
one who does not love does not know God, for God is love" (1 John 4:8). God indwells
every believer and never departs.

Do you not know that you are a temple of God, and that the Spirit of God dwells in
you? (1 Cor. 3:16)

I will never desert you, nor will I ever forsake you. (Heb. 13:5b)

The love that God is, is always within us. Albeit at times, we cannot feel love because
it may be repressed deeply underneath the hurt.

The negative feelings toward another must be put away. They are to be replaced
with feelings of love and kindness.

Let all bitterness and wrath and anger and clamor and slander be put away from you,
along with all malice. And be kind to one another, tender-hearted, forgiving each other,
just as God in Christ also has forgiven you. (Eph. 4:31–32, see also Col. 3:12–14)

Conflictual relationships are revealing tests of Christian maturity and discipleship.
Jesus taught in the Sermon on the Mount, that loving the unloving and undeserving is
a basic characteristic in knowing and loving Him.

But I say to you who hear, love your enemies, do good to those who hate you, bless
those who curse you, pray for those who mistreat you. . . . And if you love those who
love you, what credit is that to you? For even sinners love those who love them. And

if you do good to those who do good to you, what credit is that to you? For even sinners do the same thing . . . But love your enemies, and do good and lend, expecting nothing in return; and your reward will be great, and you will be sons of the Most High; for He Himself is kind to the ungrateful and evil men. Be merciful, just as your Father is merciful. (Luke 6:27–28; 32–33; 35–36)

A clear test for how much we love God, the One who has loved us unconditionally, is revealed when we choose to release His love to others who have hurt us. Loving God is obeying God's commandments. "If you love Me, you will keep My commandments" (John 14:15). The unwillingness to love others reflects a compromised love for God.

A new commandment I give to you, that you love one another, even as I have loved you, that you love one another. (John 13:34)

This is a commandment, not a suggestion. Unjust or abusive circumstances do not reduce God's firm commandment to a suggested response. We are commanded to love with His love.

It is outright disobedience to Almighty God, when we withhold His love within us. It is crucial that we remember how much God has loved us in spite of our sinfulness.

How much has God loved us? Consider the following verses.

John 3:16 *He required His Son to die for our sins. And has given us eternal life.*
Romans 6:23, 2 Thessalonians 1:8–9 *We have been spared eternal judgment in hell.*
Romans 5:8, 10 *God loved us unconditionally, even as His enemies.*

LEADER'S SECTION

Teacher's Worksheet

"See *how great a love* the Father has *bestowed upon us,* that we should be called children of God" (1 John 3:1a).

God's great love: John 3:16; Romans 6:23; 2 Thessalonians 1:8–9; Romans 5:8, 10; 1 Corinthians 13:4–8a.

Reflect on how great a love we have received from God.
1. After having His love "bestowed upon us," what did we also receive?
  1 John 3:24b *the Holy Spirit indwelt us*
  1 John 4:8 *the love of God indwelt us*
  Galatians 5:22–23 *the fruit of the Spirit within us*
2. What are we suppose to do in return?

  1 John 4:20–21; 5:2–3 *love God and obey His commandments without compulsion*
  1 John 3:16 *love one another with total self-sacrifice*
  1 John 4:17 *reflect/model (perfect) the love of God*
3. How can we actually love with God's love?
  1 John 3:24; 4:16 *by abiding in God*

4. If abiding is the secret, how do we "abide in Him?"

1 John 3:24 *by keeping His commandments, purpose in your heart to obey*

1 John 4:16, 21 *purpose in your heart to love by releasing God and His love*

1 John 1:5–7; 3:6 *maintain intimate fellowship with God, by being cleansed of all sins*

When we are in fellowship with God (in regular communion with Him), He fills us with His desires and power (Phil. 2:13).

5. What is the basic problem when we do not extend love to others?
Sin, an unwillingness to abide in Him and obey His commandments.

It is a serious sin to withhold God and His love through you, to others. We block the flow of His love by harboring anger, resentment, bitterness, unforgive- ness, and hurts. These negative emotions are poisonous to relationships! Obviously, fellowship with God has been broken (1 John 1:5–7, Isa. 59:2).

6. What must we do to be freed from this condition, and restore fellowship with God?

Revelation 2:4–5 *recount where we have fallen, repent and release God's love again*

1 John 1:9 *acknowledge or confess this terrible sin of withholding God's love*

7. Why do we choose to withhold God's love?
We feel offended, angry, resentful, and are fearful of hurt and rejection. We don't feel love anymore and have decided that the person is no longer deserving.

The ultimate expression of our love for

ANGER   RESENTMENT

HURT   SADNESS

DISAPPOINTMENT

FEAR   INSECURITIES

WOUNDEDNESS

Negative Emotions

God, is the releasing of His love to people when they are undeserving and unlovely (Luke 6:22–23; 27–28; 32–36). God's love is perfected when it is allowed to run its course to the undeserving and unlovely.

When relationships are strained or damaged by oppressive negative emotions, God's love is suppressed. The choice to withhold God's love leads to a broken fellowship with God. "Abiding in Him" becomes impossible. There is a disconnection from the desires and power of God.

How to Replace Negative Emotions with God's Love

1. Be honest with yourself and God. Are there any hurtful ways in me? (Psalm 139:23–24)

anger—Eph. 4:26–31

hurt—Col. 3:13; Matt. 18:21–34

fear—Phil. 4:6–7; 1 Peter 5:7

Have any of these feelings led you toward hurtful ways?

2. Confess and repent. Receive God's forgiveness, and be restored in your fellowship with Him (Rev. 2:4–5; 1 John 1:9).

3. Ask God to give you a clean heart and to fill it with His love (Psalm 51:10).

4. Now you can "abide in Him" and release His love (1 John 4:16).

*See Appendix C, Student Worksheet

AGAPE LOVE

FORGIVENESS

FRUIT OF THE SPIRIT
("Love, joy, peace. . . . ")

A Clean Heart

CHAPTER 4

FORGIVENESS: KEY TO RESTORING RELATIONSHIPS

Bearing with one another, and forgiving each other, whoever has a complaint against any one; just as the Lord forgave you, so also should you. (Col. 3:13)

RELATIONSHIPS DON'T JUST HAPPEN BY CHANCE. THE SOVEREIGNTY OF GOD brings people together in love and communion. God designs relationships. We certainly believe this about Christian marriages. The wedding ceremony is the celebration of a union "made in heaven." Jesus affirmed this truth in Matthew 19:6b, "What God has joined together, let no man separate."

In their wedding vows, the bride and groom acknowledged the sanctity of marriage. "With God as your witness, will you promise to love, honor, respect, and serve her/him, in sickness and in health, in adversity and in prosperity, for better or for worse, so long as you both shall live?" "Yes!" The commitment was made for life!

When a husband or wife chooses to sever the marriage relationship, God's handiwork is trashed. His will is subverted. What an affront to Almighty God. Where is the fear of God?

Similarly, through God's Sovereignty, He brings believers together in a community to unite into a local church fellowship. "But now God has placed the members, each one of them, in the body, just as He desired" (1 Cor. 12:18). The apostle Paul also recognized God's handiwork in local church membership.

> But God so composed the body . . . , that there should be no division in the body, but that the members should give the same care for one another. (1 Cor. 12:24–25)

Utmost care should be given to guard the unity of the fellowship. Divisiveness and broken relationships are totally out of God's will. We must be busy about the "ministry of reconciliation" (2 Cor. 5:18).

The Holy Spirit desires to restore broken relationships. His power and love can reconcile any relationship. God is always ready to do His part. The unreconciled must be willing to do their part. There must be a willingness to forgive. Forgiveness is the key to initiate the reconciliation process.

All feelings within you may resist the thought of forgiving someone who has hurt you deeply. A woman once told me, "It never crossed my mind to forgive that person for what he did." You might say, "You don't know how much that person hurt me!" I would add, "Without forgiving, you allow that person to continue hurting you."

Forgiveness lets the other person off the hook. But it also gets you off their hook, and releases you from the pain of the past connected to that person. This is God's will for every relationship. The thread of forgiveness weaves throughout the Bible. Joseph forgave his brothers for abusing him.

> Thus you shall say to Joseph, "Please forgive, I beg you, the transgression of your brothers and their sin, for they did you wrong." . . . And Joseph wept when they spoke to him. (Gen. 50:17)

God told the prophet Hosea to repurchase Gomer the harlot, and take her back as his wife. Even though she had defiled herself in sexual unfaithfulness. (Hos. 3:1–3) In Luke chapter fifteen, the Prodigal Son receives complete forgiveness from his father. The ultimate display of forgiveness was Jesus on the cross, "Father forgive them; for they do not know what they are doing" (Luke 23:34). Jesus forgave His enemies to make possible a reconciliation.

> For if while we were enemies, we were reconciled to God through the death of His Son, much more, having been reconciled, we shall be saved by His life. (Rom. 5:10)

Christians, as disciples of Jesus, are to live out the life and message of Jesus. This requires obedience to His commandments. "But I say to you, love your enemies, and pray for those who persecute you" (Matt. 5:44). This is radical love, but is to be the normal standard for a Christian.

In God's kingdom, where He is Lord, the forgiven is to bless the enemy or wrong doer with forgiveness.

> Then summoning him, his lord said to him, "You wicked slave, I forgave you all that debt because you entreated me. Should you not also have had mercy on your fellow slave, even as I had mercy on you?" (Matt. 18:32–33)

Lewis Smedes makes some very insightful statements about forgiveness (*The Art of Forgiving,* Lewis B. Smedes, 177–78).

> The most creative power given to the human spirit is the power to heal the wounds of a past it cannot change.

> The first person to benefit from forgiving is the one who does it.

> We forgive people only for what they do, never for who they are.

> Forgiving is a journey; the deeper the wound, the longer the journey.

> Waiting for someone to repent before we forgive is to surrender our future to the person that has wronged us.

> When we forgive, we set a prisoner free and discover that the prisoner we set free is us.

LEADER'S SECTION

Teacher's Worksheet

The resistance to forgive is humanly instinctive. It's understandable. Our sense of justice concludes that the hurtful person doesn't deserve forgiveness. Especially if that person doesn't even recognize their wrongdoing.

Our forgiveness was not deserved either. We desperately needed God's forgiveness and are so glad we have received it! Since God commanded that we forgive, the issue of forgiving is more about our relationship with God, than it is with the other person.

The decision to *not* forgive, is a choice to not obey God. This is willful sin. Share what these verses say about sin and forgiveness.

1. *A willful sinner is out of fellowship with God* (Isa. 59:2; 1 John 1:6–7).
2. *Unforgiveness is unconfessed sin* (1 John 1:9).
3. *God commands His followers to forgive* (Matt. 18:23–35; Eph. 4:32; Col. 3:13).
4. *We are to forgive even if there is no repentance* (Luke 23:34). You don't need the other person's cooperation. Sometimes, they are already dead or unavailable. Forgiving brings inner healing to the forgiver and insures a right relationship with God.
5. *Leave the person being forgiven in God's hands* (Rom. 12:17–19).
6. *There is no limit as to how often one has to forgive* (Matt. 18:21–22).
7. *Whether you are the victim or offender, God expects you to initiate the reconciliation* (Matt. 5:23–24; 18:15; Rom. 12:18). It is always your turn. God just wants to get it accomplished. It is too important to God, to be waiting on the other. In many cases, reconciliation would never happen.
8. *Harboring an unforgiving spirit gives the devil entry to affect the quality of your life and relationships* (2 Cor. 2:10–11).

Forgiving from the Heart

1. Decide to forgive in obedience to the Lord. Leave the justice to God. Forgiveness is working on resolving your pain, and leaving the other person to God.
2. Set aside one to two hours for unhurried time alone with God. Ask God to reveal all those who have hurt or offended you. Make a list of these names.
3. Let God search the depths of your heart. To forgive from the heart, you must face the hurt, anger, bitterness, or hatred.
4. Take your list of names. For each person on the list, pray aloud. Take your time. "Lord God, I forgive *(name)* for (whatever has hurt or angered you), which made me feel *(feelings)*. I choose to forgive (name), and I leave him/her in your hands."
5. Destroy the list. Thank God for your inner freedom. Your forgiveness is between you and God. There is no need to tell the other persons, unless they have asked you for forgiveness.
6. The healing will take time. The time will come when you will be able to think of them without feeling hurt or anger.

★See Appendix D, Student Worksheet.

UNIT II

RESOLVING CONFLICTS
IN THE CHURCH

CHAPTER 5

CONFLICT IN THE CHURCH

Now I exhort you, brethren, by the name of the Lord Jesus Christ, that you all agree, and there be no divisions among you, but be made complete in the same mind and in the same judgment. (1 Cor. 1:10)

C HURCH CONFLICT IS A SERIOUS PROBLEM TODAY. CHURCH MEMBERS ARE leaving their churches disgruntled and hurt over internal strife. Churches have split over unresolved conflicts. When I am called upon to mediate church conflict, it always grieves me to see God's people feeling such anger, hurt and hopelessness. Some tell me that they dread going to church because of the tension and offensiveness. It is appalling to observe the destructiveness of unresolved conflict in the church.

One person described how some members will walk by with no acknowledgment and with stonefaces. They want everyone to know that they are mad and unhappy about church affairs, sitting with this disposition during the worship service. She said she didn't dare invite anyone to her church to visit. Can you imagine? She didn't want her friends to get turned off to Christ by visiting her church!

Churches in conflict may have power struggles, stormy business meetings, gossiping, backbiting and other hurtful actions. There may be confusion over the proper roles of leaders and just who is in charge of what. The members become increasingly frustrated over happenings at church, and the "un-Christian" behavior of members, especially of some leaders.

All of the negative feelings generated in a conflictual church create an environment for divisiveness and disunity. The people grow intolerant. Forced termination of the pastor is often the outcome. Recently, I counseled with a pastor who was fired and given no severance pay. This action was inexcusable. Everyone loses and God is dishonored. In far too many cases, the church is known in its community more for its problems and unrest, than for its fellowship of love.

The witness of God is at stake. The very mission of the church can be sabotaged by the unloving behavior of its members. To tolerate hurtful and divisive actions in church life is a serious sin. Church experience should provide an atmosphere of joy, peace, and love. Life is tough enough outside of the church.

Church conflict is not new. The Book of Acts records conflict in the very first Christian church.

Now at this time while the disciples were increasing in number, a complaint arose on the part of the Hellenistic Jews against the native Hebrews, because their widows were being overlooked in the daily serving of food. (Acts 6:1)

The Apostle Paul also identified the problem in the church of Corinth.

> Now I exhort you, brethren, by the name of our Lord Jesus Christ, that you all agree, and there be no divisions among you, but you be made complete in the same mind and in the same judgment. For I have been informed concerning you, my brethren, by Chloe's people, that there are quarrels among you. (1 Cor. 1:10–11)

In the next chapter, I will delineate how to resolve conflicts in a God-honoring way, based on biblical principles. For biblical resolution, it is necessary to identify the hurtful attitudes and actions as sins.

In 2 Corinthians 12:20–21a, Paul referred to such behaviors as sins that needed repentance. "For I am afraid that perhaps when I come I may find you to be not what I wish and may be found by you to be not what you wish; that perhaps there may be strife, jealousy, angry tempers, disputes, slanders, gossip, arrogance, disturbances; I am afraid that when I come again my God may humiliate me before you, and I may mourn over many of those who have sinned in the past and not repented. . . . "

Mourning is the appropriate response for sin in the church fellowship. A sin problem is a spiritual problem. Thus, Biblical conflict resolution will necessitate God's intervention to bring healing and the cleansing of all unrighteousness. It will require individual and corporate repentance from God's people.

Church leadership has been remiss to treat the problem as a spiritual one. Often times, the problems are ignored. I get so irritated when I hear a church leader say, "Let's just forget the past and move on to the future." Some churches have generations of unresolved problems. A new pastor comes and he doesn't have a clue what hit him! Sometimes he finds himself paying for sins of the past. No wonder pastors are not staying more than a few years on the average.

Some conflicted churches will terminate their pastor, some members will leave because of this action, and the church will proceed forward without missing a beat. They conclude that the problems are gone. What arrogance!

What about all the hurt that was inflicted during the conflict? What about the broken relationships? What about all the ill feelings and woundedness? What about the new Christians that are now disillusioned and damaged spiritually? What about the dishonoring of God and the witness of the church? What about all of the sins that go unconfessed?

I have been in several churches where the conflicts aren't that open, but the evidence is more on a passive-aggressive level. The congregation exhibits some of the following characteristics: lack of trust, guardedness, feelings that are easily hurt, little risk-taking, reserved involvement, fear of being hurt or criticized, avoidance of conflict, pessimism, depressive worship, uncommittedness, sporadic joy, people leaving without notice, lack of humor, small core of controlling leaders, aversion to inviting friends, and no church growth. Like the Apostle Paul, it is time to mourn!

Could God be holding back revival in America because of the unrecognized hurtful sins and arrogant attitudes?

> And My people who are called by My name humble themselves and pray, and seek My face and turn from their wicked ways, then I will hear from heaven, will forgive their sin, and will heal their land. (2 Chron. 7:14)

Case Study: First Baptist Church, Anycity

The church called a new pastor with a unanimous vote. The congregation was very excited and hopeful about the future. The attendance had plateaued over the years and the median age had increased to fifty-five years of age.

The new pastor was young, married and had two small children. The church realized that it must reach young families to insure a growing church in the future. In the first year, several new young families were reached. This growth created an initial excitement and encouraged visionary leadership.

The pastor scheduled a leadership retreat to get more intentional with future goals for growth. He excitedly shared a number of new ideas and recommended several changes. He was adamant that the worship service needed more upbeat music to continue to attract the younger crowd. The young adults at the retreat agreed enthusiastically.

The older members were more reserved with their agreement. Some shared that they wanted to reach the unchurched but that the changes should be done slowly and not recklessly. This was interpreted by some to indicate that the older members were going to resist change.

The retreat ended with an apparent lack of unity. The pastor sensed frustration and discouragement among some of the newer members. The pastor began to socialize more with the younger adults as they affirmed his ideas for changes.

The older members and the longtime leaders felt somewhat alienated and put aside. They were not being consulted by the pastor like he used to approach them for advice. They began to have feelings of mistrust. People began to spread their discontent and church concerns through gossip.

Divisiveness was setting into the fellowship. The opinions became emotionally charged and feelings were hurt. Backbiting and blame became common. This negative spirit was manifested in business meetings. There were sarcastic comments, accusations, and outbursts of anger. Many were embarrassed at the hurtful attitudes and actions. A spirit of discouragement and frustration was evident in the fellowship. Even in the worship service, some would not participate and sat with arms crossed and stone faces.

Church is where Christlike love and kindness is suppose to be the standard or hallmark of behavior. Attendance began to fade, some resigned from their leadership positions, and some families left with disgust.

The pastor was very irritated and frustrated with those that were resisting his leadership. He felt like leaving also, desiring to pastor a people that would be more cooperative. Since the pastor was the spiritual leader, he felt that he had to start speaking out against the resistance to change for the sake of reaching the unchurched. Some accused him of using the pulpit as a bully whip.

The church was in a major crisis. The church was in conflict.

LEADER'S SECTION

Teacher's Worksheet

The church in conflict has lost its spiritual focus. Many begin to engage in actions to save the church from those they blame for the negativity. There is disunity of spirit and damaged relationships. There is distrust and disrespect for the leadership.

The church must return to the Biblical foundations for church life. State a principle from each of the scriptural foundations.

1. Colossians 1:18 *Jesus Christ is the head of the church. His will is supreme.*
2. 1 Corinthians 12:14–27 *God places each person in the body and all are equally important to Him.*
3. Ephesians 5:25 *Jesus loves the church more than any leader in the church.*
4. Colossians 1:22 *Jesus' goal is to present His body as holy, blameless, and beyond reproach. Who we are is more important than what we do.*
5. John 17:20–23, 26 *All relationships in the church are to be ruled by love and unity.*
6 Matthew 18:15–17 *Jesus outlined His conflict resolution procedure for the church.*
7. Ephesians 4:1–4, 15–16, 25–32; Colossians 3:12–15; 1 Corinthians 1:10 *Hurtful or offensive actions, divisions and disunity are scriptural violations of God's guidelines for relating in the church.*
8. Matthew 5:23–24; 2 Corinthians 5:18 *Reconciliation begins with one's relationship to God, followed by reconciliation to fellow Christians.*
9. 1 John 1:6–9; 2 Chronicles 7:14 *The disobedience and hurtful actions are sins allowed in the church. Personal and corporate repentance is necessary to restore fellowship with God. Healing and revival only come after repentance.*

*See Appendix E, Student Worksheet

CHAPTER 6

CHURCH CONFLICT RESOLUTION PROCESS

And if your brother sins, go and reprove him in private, if he listens to you, you have won your brother. But if he doesn't listen to you, take one or two more with you, so that by the mouth of two or three witnesses every fact may be confirmed. (Matt. 18:15–16)

THE PREVIOUS CHAPTER HIGHLIGHTED THE NEGATIVE AND DESTRUCTIVE effects of church conflict. The conflictual condition is created by the compounding of unrestrained sins within the church fellowship. The problem is spiritual and requires a spiritual remedy.

Church conflict needs to be handled as a spiritual conflict. The true enemy of the church is the devil. He thrives like a weed in a fertile environment of church conflict.

Phase one of the resolution process focuses on the Lordship of Christ, and the acknowledgment of responsibility to conduct church life in godliness. The quality of church life must reflect the glory of God and not the glory of the devil. It is so grievous to God when the church fails and tolerates behaviors that glorify the adversary. This phase is intended to reconcile the church and Christ, the Head of the church, in right relationship.

Phase two is intended to reconcile relationships within the church fellowship. The process identifies the major issues of contention and leads to corrective actions with a redemptive spirit.

Phase One: Submission to the Lordship of Christ

1. Have the church leadership take a spiritual inventory of the church life.
Spiritual Inventory of Church Fellowship

__Outbursts of anger	__Spiritual apathy	__Chaos, confusion
__Backbiting slander	__Mistrust	__Bitterness, animosity
__Gossip	__Divisiveness,	__Worldliness
__Hurtful jesting	contentiousness	__Arrogant pride
__Rudeness, disrespect	__Dishonesty,	__Members leaving
__Strained relationships	deception	__Unwillingness
__Exclusivity, cliques	__Immorality	to forgive

2. The church leadership should discuss and agree upon the seriousness of their corporate spiritual condition. (No blaming!)

It is crucial to appraise the negative impact of the fellowship sins. Relationships may be strained or severed. There may be chaos, anarchy, and divisiveness. The witness of Christ and His love may have been disgraced.

The church leadership is responsible for protecting the fellowship from harm. The sins of the members must no longer be tolerated or ignored. The apostle Paul chastened the church at Corinth for tolerating sin. He exhorted them to rather mourn over such behavior among the people of God (1 Cor. 5:1–8; 2 Cor. 12:20–21). There must be a facilitation of both individual and corporate repentance.

3. Call the church to a prayer alert or Solemn Assembly.
   Scriptural Foundation: Joel 1:13–14; 2:12–17; Psalm 51:1–17; James 5:16; 2 Chronicles 7:11–16
   Objective: To assemble the church in a prayerful and humble state, seeking personal and corporate repentance, giving the Holy Spirit an opportunity to minister restoration to the body of Christ, and crown Jesus as the Lord of His church.
   Process: Seek God's face • Cleansed hearts • Repentance • Heal spiritual brokenness • Restored relationships • Healing of hurts • Unity of congregation
   Plan of Action:
   1. Schedule a day of prayer for either the church leaders or the whole congregation.
   2. The Solemn Assembly should be led by an outside facilitator, if the pastor is involved in the issues of conflict.
   [Note: Materials on Solemn Assembly can be ordered from International Awakening Press, P.O. Box 232, Wheaton, Illinois 60189; (630) 653-8616.]

Phase Two: Resolution of Conflict among the Members

This phase is usually most effective when the church votes to call upon an outside facilitator. The vote is necessary to confer a spiritual leadership role upon the outsider. Since the church is autonomous, no outsider has any authority except granted as a privilege, by the congregation. His role would be to lead the church in a God-honoring process to restore unity in the body.
   Scriptural Foundation: 1 Corinthians 1:10; Matthew 5:23–4; Matthew 18:15–17, John 8:32; 17:22–23; Ephesians 4:1–3
   Objective: To clarify the issues of conflict, leading the church to resolve the issues in a redemptive process, restoring the unity of the spirit and the reconciliation of relationships.
   Plan of Action:
   1. Schedule the dates to conduct the conflict resolution process (three meetings).
      a. Preach and give an overview of the process.
      b. Meet with various leadership groups to gain their perspectives of the issues.
      c. Report summary: Evaluation and Recommendations (★See Appendix J)
   [Note: At times, there are relationships that need immediate reconciliation. Private meetings following the procedure in Matthew 18:15-17, may be necessary (★ See Appendix I).]
   2. Distribute the Congregational Questionnaire to all active members.

The questionnaire is to be returned directly to the church consultant and remains completely confidential. The information is only for the consultant. His evaluation and recommendations will factor heavily from the whole congregation's input. The goal is for God to speak through the whole body, to the whole body. This is a truth validation process to dispel half-truths and exaggerations. The intent is for everyone to respond to the exact same body of information (the consultant's findings), and not what they have heard on the "grapevine" (★ See Appendix H).

3. The consultant will summarize the findings, identify the violations of Scripture and Church Constitution and Bylaws, and the major issues of conflict and the contributing factors.

4. The consultant will submit a written report of his evaluation and recommendations. They will include corrective actions that will insure future protection of the unity of the fellowship, and the healthy resolution of conflict in a timely, orderly, and God-honoring way.

LEADER'S SECTION

Teacher's Worksheet

Jesus gave clear step-by-step instructions on how to righteously resolve conflicts among Christians. His instructions can be found in Matthew 5:23–24; 18:15–17. When this biblical procedure is followed with a redemptive and loving spirit, He confers heavenly authority on the decision of the church, and promises His powerful presence (Matt. 18:18–20).

1. If you have offended someone, you should go to him in private and seek to be reconciled to him (Matt. 5:23–24).

2. Reconciliation is foremost on God's priority list (Matt. 5:23–24; 2 Cor. 5:18). Reconciliation is the core message of the Bible, man with God and with each other.

Before going to confront someone, consider the following principles.

a. Examine yourself before God (Ps. 139:23–24).

Do I have any unconfessed sin? Have I offended him? Have I failed to be a Christlike example? Have I considered how I can help him overcome the problem?

b. Scrutinize your wording to be non-offensive.

"I have decided that I will only share positive information about you to anyone who asks. For this reason I wonder if you could help me explain something I am not sure I understand."

"Have I done something wrong to cause you to react in this way?"

"I have had a problem in the past with this area . . . "

c. Search out your resistance to going to him and confronting him in private.

•Your own sins prevent you.

•You have already told it to others.

•Your pride prevents you from revealing that he was able to hurt you.

•Procrastination.

•Doubt. You don't believe it will do any good. You tried it before. Warning: Don't exalt your experience over the Lord's command.

•Ignorance. Now you are no longer ignorant of Jesus' instruction.

d. Check your motive. Commit yourself to only giving a good report of others, unless you have followed the steps of Matthew chapter eighteen, and in the right spirit.

3. If someone has offended you, you should *go to him in private and share specifically what was done that offended you. This*

should be done in private to guard his dignity, treating him with the respect and value that God extends to all His children. The goal is to *restore and help the brother,* not hurt him (Matt. 18:15). The test of spirituality is not to expose sin, but to restore the sinner.

4. It is at this juncture that most Christians falter. Instead of talking secretly to the offender, the offendee talks secretly to others about the offender.

This is sin! It is a sin against God's Word and against your brother. God hates gossip. However, the devil loves gossip because it is through this channel that he spreads ill feelings, distortions, and discord. Gossip in the church is so prevalent that I felt a strong need to provide a separate study on this destructive sin in the church (★ See Appendix K).

If you are not directly the offended one, the Bible gives instruction to become involved to help the brother who has fallen (Gal. 6:1).

5. If the sinner does not repent, then Jesus gives instruction to widen the appeal to a *few witnesses* (Matt. 18:16).

The witnesses can be verifiers of the truth about the allegation(s), or serve as witnesses to whether he repents or not. The meeting is to be confidential. If the sinner repents, but others have already heard about his sins, his reputation is unfairly and unnecessarily hurt. "Therefore whatever you want others to do for you, do so for them" (Matt. 7:12). The reputation of the repentant sinner is not to be previously maligned.

6. If after meeting with a small group, there is still no repentance or resolution, then the matter must be brought forward for the church to resolve. Hopefully, this public scrutiny will motivate repentance. If not, church discipline must follow. Most churches disobey Christ and don't carry out this final step. Chapter seven will provide guidelines for carrying out church discipline. Church discipline should be done with a redemptive spirit, and only as a last measure.

★See Appendix F, Student Worksheet

CHAPTER 7

CHURCH DISCIPLINE FOR THE UNREPENTANT

And if he refuses to listen to the them, tell it to the church; and if he refuses to listen even to the church, let him be to you as a Gentile and a tax-gatherer. (Matt. 18:17)

IN MY ROLE AS A CHURCH CONFLICT MEDIATOR, I REGULARLY OBSERVE A weakened condition in these conflicted churches. They are plagued with problems such as factions, tension, open display of hurtful behavior and attitudes, power struggles, anarchy, withholding of tithes, unwillingness to serve, and lack of trust in the leadership. This environment destroys unity.

The glue that holds a congregation in unity is Christ's peace and love.

And beyond all these things put on love, which is the perfect bond of unity. And let the peace of Christ rule in your hearts, to which indeed you were called in one body; and be thankful. (Col. 3:14–15)

When there is an absence of love and peace, the church is easily fragmented. Members are prone to leave disgusted, hurting, and resentful. I can understand why they leave. Some have told me "I wouldn't dare invite someone to my church. I wouldn't want them to be turned off to Christ." "I couldn't take it anymore." "There is no leadership in this church." "I don't understand why somebody doesn't do something about those people."

This identifies a common thread among conflicted churches. There is a frustration with the inaction of the church to deal with sins within the body. So I understand why good people finally give up and leave. But leaving is not the proper biblical response, unless God has indeed called them elsewhere. Every member is responsible to insist on biblical action for problems within the fellowship.

It is a biblical requirement of the church to follow Jesus' clear instructions to eradicate sin and restrain sinners in the church. But most churches seem reluctant to carry out church discipline. These same churches will unreservedly affirm the authority of Scripture, but ignore the Scriptural injunction for church discipline, and not hold members accountable to repent for ungodly behavior.

The church leaders are responsible to guard the honor of Christ. His name is blasphemed when ungodliness is tolerated in church life. It is so disgraceful when a church's "claim to fame" is divisiveness, hurtfulness and power struggles. Business meetings are notorious for "fussing and fighting." Church members are bewildered as to why this fleshly behavior is tolerated.

The church leaders are also responsible to protect the fellowship from harm. In a conflicted church, people are being hurt regularly. They are not protected from gossip, backbiting, tension, and even open warfare. People act mean, say sarcastic things, and there is no accountability for their actions. The church was to be a refuge from the world's troubles, but in conflicted churches it is a battlefield. When is someone going to do something?

Why are churches reluctant to engage in church discipline? Some are fearful of dividing the church or losing members. Others lack courage and are avoidant of conflict. There is reluctance to be the "bad guy" or have the blood on their hands. Yet, others don't want to hurt or offend the troublemaker!

Some churches simply do not know what to do. When should church discipline be exercised? What warrants church discipline? How should it be carried out?

⟪━━⟫

LEADER'S SECTION

Teacher's Worksheet

Why should the church be diligent to carry out church discipline?

To neglect church discipline is clear disobedience to God's Word (Matt. 18:17; 1 Cor. 5:1–13; Titus 3:10–11; Rom. 16:17).

Church discipline should be exercised . . .

1. *to eradicate sin in the fellowship and its damaging effects* (1 Cor. 5:1–13).

2. *to instill the fear of God and deter other's involvement in sinful behavior* (1 Tim. 5:20).

3. *to silence false teachers and their influence in the church* (Titus 1:10–11).

4. *to restore and correct a sinning believer* (Gal. 6:1; Heb. 12:10–13; James 5:20; 2 Thess. 3:14–15).

5. *to guard the testimony of God and His church* (2 Sam. 12:14; 1 Peter 1:14; 2:9).

6. *to protect the community of believers from harm* (Acts 20:28; Gal. 5:16).

7. *to produce people with a healthy faith* (Titus 1:13).

8. *to encourage spiritual healing* (Heb. 12:10–13).

[Note: *See Appendix G, Student Worksheet.]

Church Discipline Guidelines

The goal in the church discipline process is to bring the wayward believer to repentance and restoration. It is intended to be corrective and restorative, rather than punitive.

Biblical church discipline is God's ordained process for the church to intervene and squelch sin and its harmful effects in the fellowship of the church. God entrusted the church with the authority and responsibility to carry out this spiritual discipline (Matt. 18:17–19; 1 Cor. 5:12–13).

The apostle Paul directed the churches in Corinth and Thessalonica to take disciplinary action against the wayward believers (1 Cor. 5:1–13; 2 Thess. 3:6–15). He was very adamant about the church maintaining a pure fellowship and taking sin seriously.

Discipline is not easy to do. It is difficult to do it correctly. Courage and knowledge are necessary; courage to face rebuke and criticism, and knowledge of how to properly exercise biblical church discipline.

According to Hebrews 12:5-11, discipline is God's strategy to help His followers mature and grow in righteousness. The church must not withhold this blessing from an erring believer.

Excommunication or disfellowshipping may seem harsh or too radical. It cannot be overemphasized that at each stage in the process, restoration is the goal. Even after a member is disfellowshipped, the church is instructed to continue reaching out for restoration to God and the church (2 Cor. 2:5–9).

The church leadership must exemplify a redemptive spirit of love and concern. The unrepentant believer will invite God's wrath (Heb. 10:26–31). The church should mourn with regret as she exhorts with a spirit of gentleness. What a terrible plight to be in. Repentance and restoration should be encouraged throughout the process (Gal. 6:1–2; 2 Tim. 2:25–26; 2 Cor. 12:20–21).

Don't shoot the wounded! (Matt. 18:13; Gal. 6:1–2).

Procedures For Church Discipline

And if your brother sins, go and reprove him in private; if he listens to you, you have won your brother. But if he doesn't listen to you, take one or two more with you, so that "By the mouth of two or three witnesses every fact may be confirmed." And if he refuses to listen to them, tell it to the church; and if he refuses to listen even to the church, *let him be to you as a Gentile or tax-gatherer.* (italics for emphasis, Matt. 18:15-17)

God's corrective process begins with a *private* one-on-one appeal for repentance. Then it is strengthened with a *private* small group appeal. Finally, it is strengthened with a *public* large group appeal. If he still refuses to repent, excommunication must follow.

Truly I say to you, whatever you shall bind on earth shall have been bound in heaven; and whatever you loose on earth shall have been loosed in heaven. Again I say to you, that if two of you agree on earth about anything that they may ask, it shall be done for them by My Father who is in heaven. For where two or three have gathered in My name, there I am in their midst. (Matt. 18:18–20)

These verses underscore God's directive to the church to prayerfully seek His will through consensus and unanimity. He affirms it with heavenly authority and His presence. Each stage in the process must be bathed in much prayer.

1. *"tell it to the church"*

In a congregational governed church (eg. Baptist), the appropriate body of leaders would make a public announcement about the situation, review the procedures that were followed for restoration, and a recommendation for disfellowship, if there is no immediate repentance.

In a special called business session, the congregation would vote their will. The necessary majority vote should be noted from the Church Constitution and Bylaws. If there isn't any specific reference, then a simple majority vote (51%) would be sufficient for the action. Hopefully, after much prayer, there would be a unanimous vote.

In a elder governed church (eg. Presbyterian), the elders would follow the same procedures in making the issue public about the church discipline. However, the difference would be the action to disfellowship, if no immediate repentance, would be their decision and not a recommendation for congregational vote. This is assuming that their bylaws do not specifically instruct otherwise.

Carl Laney relates a story about the tragic results of a church that neglected its duty for church discipline. A single woman in the church became pregnant. Some heard that she was going to have an abortion. Several women confronted her and an offer was even made by one member to adopt the baby. But the woman would not change her mind.

Some went to the pastor and suggested church discipline. He was concerned that the issue would divide the church. Instead, he advocated "loving her back into the fellowship." She had the abortion and never admitted any wrongdoing. Many people left the church. "The problem is that the ones leaving are those who are sensitive to sin and desire a holy fellowship! The leaven of impurity is permeating this congregation" (Laney, *A Guide to Church Discipleship,* 59).

2. *"let him be to you as a Gentile and a tax-gatherer"*

They were considered outsiders and unbelievers. Jesus advocated treating them as outsiders since they did not heed the authority of Christ and the church. The apostle Paul instructed the church to "avoid" and "remove" the unrepentant sinner (1 Cor. 5:11, 13; 2 Thess. 3:6, 14).

Restoration is the goal at every stage. After a member is disfellowshipped, the church should still follow up and reach out with loving appeals (2 Cor. 2:6–9). How did Jesus treat the Gentiles and tax gatherers? He reached out to them with love, leading them to get right with God (Matt. 9:9–13).

How does your church presently reach out to outsiders? The disfellowshipped member should continue to be the recipient of the church's love and appeal to get right with God.

If there is repentance, then the church should forgive and restore to fellowship and membership (Luke 17:4). The whole process of church discipline is to be overshadowed with a redemptive spirit.

Jay Adams (*Handbook of Church Discipline,* 91) offers solid guidance on this point. "The process of restoration is set forth in II Corinthians 2. Among other things, three factors stand out:

1. The repentant offender must be forgiven.

2. He must be assisted.

3. He must be reinstated in love."

This same Paul could be so tough on sin, "Remove the wicked man from among yourselves" (1 Cor. 5:13), but tenderly with grace. "Sufficient for such a one is this punishment which was inflicted by the majority, so that on the contrary you should rather forgive and comfort him, lest somehow such a one be overwhelmed by excessive sorrow. Wherefore I urge you to reaffirm your love for him" (2 Cor. 2:6–8).

Biblical Church Discipline Process

Repentance?

```
Yes ←———— [Church member is involved in sin] ————→ No
 ↑                          |                        |
 |←———— [Private Confrontation] ————————————————————→|
 |                          |                        |
 |←———— [Private Meeting with Witnesses] ———————————→|
 |                          |                        |
 |←———— [Public Congregational Meeting] ————————————→|
 ↓                                                   ↓
[Restoration] ←————————————————————————— [Disfellowshipped]
```

•At any level, if "yes," then restoration is the next level of action.
•If "no," action proceeds to the next level of discipline.
•Restoration is still the goal, even when disfellowshipped.

CHAPTER 8

Spiritual Renewal in the Church

And My people who are called by My name will humble themselves and pray, and seek My face and turn from their wicked ways, then I will hear from heaven, will forgive their sin, and heal their land. Now My eyes shall be open and My ears attentive to the prayer offered in this place. (2 Chron. 7:14–15)

GOD HAS PROMISED TO "HEAL THE LAND" AND SEND REVIVAL. WE, THE CHURCH, are praying for revival. We are yet to fulfill the condition to turn from all wicked ways. This book has identified many sins that are being tolerated within the church fellowship.

Relationships are damaged and broken because of many sins that are committed against other Christians. The Christian home and church were to be God's lighthouses to exemplify and experience God's love and presence. Instead, far too many Christian married couples have ended in hateful divorces.

Churches have become centers of strife, exchanging angry and hurtful behavior. Many are leaving their churches in utter disgust and deep hurt. The church is suppose to be a refuge from the ungodliness of the world!

It is appalling that destructive sins are tolerated without efforts to eradicate such behavior. Where is the reverence for God? Where is the care for guarding God's reputation and the church's witness? It is time for churches to repent. There needs to be individual and corporate acknowledgment of sin and repentance.

If God's people will "turn from their wicked ways," we would see a great spiritual awakening in our day. Let it begin with you in your church.

LEADER'S SECTION

Teacher's Worksheet

Instruct the group to disperse and find a quiet place where they can pray. Assemble them back after 2-3 hours. Share your experiences. What did God say to each of you? End with a time of corporate praying.

Spiritual Self Inventory

Search me, O God, and know my heart;
Try me and know my anxious thoughts;
And see if there be any hurtful way in me,
And lead me in the everlasting way.
(Ps. 139:23–24)

Instructions: This spiritual exercise is to be used to prepare yourself for prayer, ministry, witnessing, and personal revival. Allow two to three hours for unhurried time alone with God. Give God time to search your heart and thoughts.

In reading the questions, if you are convicted of sin, write it down and confess it at once to God. Keeping a sin sheet will usually lead to a deeper cleansing experience, because it gives the Holy Spirit time to remind you of other sins connected with the ones written down. And Satan is hindered from snatching these from your thoughts.

"If we confess our sins, He is faithful and righteous to forgive us our sins and to cleanse us from all unrighteousness" (1 John 1:9). Be sure to name your sin to God, as, "Lord, I have not put you first in my plans," or "I have neglected Your Word and prayer." Do not make the least excuse for your sins.

"He who conceals his transgressions will not prosper, but he who confesses and forsakes them will find compassion" (Prov. 28:13). No matter what others do, leave nothing undone on your part. God wants to work through you to bring about a great spiritual awakening. Confession of sin will restore intimate fellowship with God, and may lead to revival among His people.

Prayerfully consider the following questions. They are intended to identify sins of omission and commission. Read the Scriptures first. Ask the questions and give a truthful answer. Every "yes" indicates a sin to be confessed and receive cleansing.

Confessional Prayer Work

1. Matthew 6:12–14. Is there anyone against whom you hold a grudge? Anyone you haven't forgiven? Anyone you hate? Anyone you refuse to love? Are there any misunderstandings that you are unwilling to forget? Is there any person against whom you are harboring bitterness, resentment, or jealousy? Anyone you dislike to hear praised? Do you allow anything to justify wrong attitudes toward others? Are there any relationships that need to be reconciled?

2. Matthew 6:33. Is there anything in which you have failed to put God first? Have your decisions been made after your own wisdom and desires, rather than seeking and following God's will? Do any of the following interfere with your surrender and service to God: ambitions, pleasures, loved ones, friendships, desire for recognition, money, your own plans?

3. Acts 1:8. Have you failed to seek the lost for Christ? Have you failed to witness consistently? Is your life failing to reveal Jesus to your friends and neighbors?

4. Galatians 5:19–21. Are you secretly pleased over the misfortune of another? Are you secretly annoyed over the accomplishments or advancement of another? Are you guilty of any unresolved contention or strife? Do you quarrel, argue or engage in heated discussions? Are you engaged in any divisions or party spirit? Do you deliberately slight some people?

5. Malachi 3:10. Have you robbed God by withholding your time, talents, and tithe? Have you failed to support mission work either in prayer or offerings?

6. 1 Corinthians 4:2. Are you undependable so you cannot be trusted with responsibilities in the Lord's work? Are you allowing your emotions to be stirred for the things of the Lord, but doing little about it?

7. 1 Corinthians 6:19–20. Are you careless with your body? Do you fail to care for it as the temple of the Holy Spirit? Are you guilty of overindulgence in eating or drinking? Do you have any habits that are defiling to the body?

8. 1 Corinthians 10:31. Do you take the slightest credit for anything good about you, rather than give all the glory to God? Do you talk of what you have done rather than what Christ has done? Do most of your sentences start with, contain, or reflect upon *I*? Have you made a pretense of being something that you are not?

9. 2 Corinthians 3:5. Are you self-conscious rather than Christ-conscious? Do you allow feelings of inferiority to keep you from attempting things in serving God?

10. Acts 24:16. Do you underpay? Do you put forth little effort in your work? Have you been careless in the payment of your debts? Do you waste time? Do you waste time for others?

11. Ephesians 4:31. Do you complain or find fault? Do you have a critical spirit toward any person or thing? Are you irritable or cranky? Do you ever carry hidden anger? Do you have outbursts of anger? Do you become impatient with others? Are you harsh, unkind, or sarcastic?

12. Ephesians 5:16. Do you listen to unedifying radio or TV programs? Do you read unworthy magazines? Do you find it necessary to seek satisfaction from any questionable source? Are you doing anything that shows you are not satisfied in the Christian walk?

13. Ephesians 5:20. Have you neglected to thank Him for all things and in all circumstances? Have you virtually called God a liar by doubting His Word? Do you worry? Is your spiritual temperature based on feelings instead of God's Word?

14. Philippians 1:21. Are you occupied with the cares of this life? Is your conversation or joy over things rather than the Lord and His Word? Does anything mean more to you than living for and pleasing God?

15. Philippians 2:14. Do you grumble or gossip? Do you speak unkindly concerning people when they are not present? Are you prejudiced against other Christians because they are of some other group or because they do not see everything as you do?

16. Philippians 4:4. Do you carry any bitterness toward God? Have you complained against Him in any way? Have you been dissatisfied with His provision? Are you unwilling to obey Him fully? Do you have any reservations as to what you would or would not do concerning anything that might be His will? Have you disobeyed some leading from Him?

17. Colossians 3:9. Do you lie? Do you exaggerate or stretch the truth?

18. 2 Timothy 2:22. Do you have personal habits that are not pure? Do you allow impure thoughts about the opposite sex to stay in your mind? Do you read material which is impure or suggest unholy things? Do you indulge in entertainment that is unclean? Are you guilty of the lustful look?

19. Hebrews 10:25. Do you stay away from the preaching of the Word? Do you whisper or think about other things during the preaching? Are you irregular in attending Bible study? Do you fail to attend prayer meetings? Have you neglected or slighted your daily private prayer time? Have you neglected God's Word? Have you neglected thanksgiving at meals? Have you neglected family devotions?

20. Hebrews 13:17. Do you fail to submit to leaders in the church or elsewhere? Do you rebel at requests given to you to help in the work of the gospel? Do you have a stubborn or unteachable spirit? Are you lazy or irresponsible?

21. James 1:27. Have you allowed yourself to become spotted by the world? Is your manner of dress pleasing to God? Do you neglect to pray about things before you buy them?

22. James 4:6. Do you feel that you are doing quite well as a Christian and that you are good enough? Are you stubborn? Do you insist on having your own way? Do you insist on your rights?

23. James 4:11. Have you dishonored Him and hindered His work by criticizing His servants? Have you failed to pray regularly for your pastor or other spiritual leaders? Do you find it hard to be corrected? Is there rebellion toward one who wants to restore you? Are you more concerned about what people will think, than what will be pleasing to God?

Remember these three things:

1. If the sin is against God, confess it to God, and accept His cleansing.

2. If the sin is against another person, confess it to God, and accept His cleansing. However, the Holy Spirit may require you to confess it to the other person before you receive a complete healing of the soul.

3. If the sin is against a group, confess it to God, and accept His cleansing. However, the Holy Spirit may require you to confess it to the group before you receive a complete healing of the soul.

If there is full confession, there will be full cleansing, and the joy of the Lord will fill one's heart. Then there can be testimony and prayer in the power of the Holy Spirit.

> Create in me a clean heart, O God, and renew a right spirit within me. . . . Restore to me the joy of Thy salvation, and sustain me with a willing spirit. Then I will teach transgressors Thy ways, and sinners will be converted to Thee. (Ps. 51:10, 12–13)

[Note: Much of this section was adapted from an anonymous handout entitled, "Heartsearcher."]

EPILOGUE

J UST AS I WAS FINISHING THIS MANUSCRIPT, I RECEIVED DISTURBING NEWS that two of my minister friends are divorcing. Distress calls come in almost weekly from pastors or church leaders, reporting major conflicts in their churches. The need is urgent!

Christians must learn biblical conflict resolution principles and the forces behind conflict. The devil is capitalizing on disunity and severed relationships among Christians. The testimony of the reality of God and His transcending love and power is at stake.

> You are the light of the world. A city set on a hill cannot be hidden. Let your light shine before men in such a way that they may see your good works, and glorify your Father who is in heaven. (Matt. 5:14, 16)

God has called us to be "ministers of reconciliation, reconciling man with God and with each other." As we approach the twenty-first century, and the soon coming of our Lord, let us be about the business of evangelizing a lost world with the gospel of peace, where the lighthouses of His love will be evident in our homes and churches. To God be the glory!

RELATIONAL CONFLICT AND EMOTIONAL/SPIRITUAL WARFARE

Student Worksheet for Chapter 1

All negative encounters in love relationships definitely need to be reframed as _____ (Eph. 5:22-6: 9; 6:11–12, 16). The devil schemes to cause difficulty in Christian relationships. The devil preys upon Christians who are wounded emotionally because they are vulnerable.

I. Identify the True Enemy
1. Satan's Nature
Matthew 4:3 _____
Revelation 12:10 _____
Revelation 12:9 _____
John 8:44b _____
1 Peter 5:8 _____
1 Corinthians 14:33 _____
Acts 10:38 _____
John 10:10a _____

Satan's nature is depicted in the Bible by the descriptive meaning of his _____. By learning his various names, it will be easy to detect when he is _____ or _____
2. Satan's mission field: _____
_____
3. Satan's strategy: _____
_____
4. Satan's goal: _____
_____

II. Consult With the Book of Life
What is a Christian instructed to do when someone is irritating, offensive, or hurtful?
Ephesians 4:15 _____

2 Timothy 2:25 _____
Matthew 18:15 _____
Matthew 5:23–24 _____
Matthew 5:44 _____
Romans 12:14, 21 _____
Colossians 3:13 _____
Colossians 3:23–24 _____
1 Peter 2:21–23 _____
Ephesians 4:31 _____
1 Kings 12:7 _____

III. Engage In Spiritual Warfare
1. 2 Corinthians 10:3–5 The weapons of our warfare are _____
_____

2. Ephesians 2:6; Revelation 4:2 Take your _____
3. Ephesians 6:11–17 Put on the _____
4. Ephesians 6:17–18; Matthew 4:1–11 Command Satan with the authority of _____
5. Romans 8:31, 37 Claim the _____
_____
6. Psalm 18:1–3 Praise God for spiritual victory. He is our _____

ANGER: MANAGE IT OR IT WILL MANAGE YOU

Student Worksheet for Chapter 2

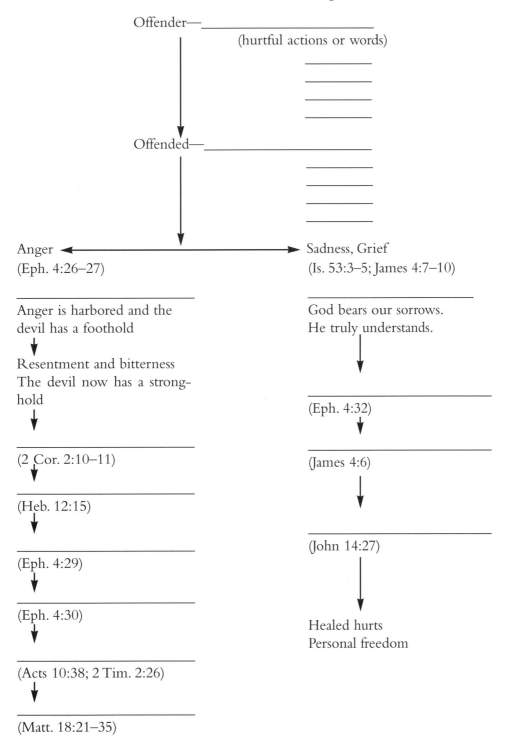

Offender—_____

(hurtful actions or words)

_____

_____

_____

_____

Offended—_____

_____

_____

_____

_____

Anger   ⟷   Sadness, Grief
(Eph. 4:26–27)   (Is. 53:3–5; James 4:7–10)

Anger is harbored and the   God bears our sorrows.
devil has a foothold   He truly understands.

Resentment and bitterness
The devil now has a stronghold

(2 Cor. 2:10–11)   (Eph. 4:32)

(Heb. 12:15)   (James 4:6)

(Eph. 4:29)

(Eph. 4:30)   (John 14:27)

(Acts 10:38; 2 Tim. 2:26)   Healed hurts
                        Personal freedom

(Matt. 18:21–35)

HEALING HURTS AND RELEASING GOD'S LOVE

Student Worksheet for Chapter 3

Reflect on how great a love we have received from God.

1. After having His love "bestowed upon us," what did we also receive?
   1 John 3:24b _____
   1 John 4:8 _____
   Galatians 5:22–23 _____

2. What are we suppose to do in return?
   1 John 4:20–21; 5:2–3 _____
   1 John 3:16 _____
   1 John 4:17 _____

3. How can we actually love with God's love?
   1 John 3:24; 4:16 _____

4. If abiding is the secret, how do we "abide in Him?"
   1 John 3:24 _____
   1 John 4:16, 21 _____
   1 John 1:5–7; 3:6 _____

When we are in fellowship with God (in regular communion with Him), He fills us with His desires and power (Phil. 2:13).

5. What is the basic problem when we do not extend love to others?

_____

_____

It is a serious sin to withhold God and His love through you, to others. We block the flow of His love by harboring anger, resentment, bitterness, unforgiveness, and hurts. These negative emotions are poisonous to relationships! Obviously, fellowship with God has been broken (1 John 1:5–7, Isa. 59:2).

6. What must we do to be freed from this condition, and restore fellowship with God?
   Revelation 2:4–5 _____
   1 John 1:9 _____

7. Why do we choose to withhold God's love?

_____

_____

_____

The ultimate expression of our love for God, is the releasing of His love to people when they are undeserving and unlovely (Luke 6:22–23; 27–28; 32–36). God's love is perfected when it is allowed to run its course to the undeserving and unlovely.

When relationships are strained or damaged by oppressive negative emotions, God's love is suppressed. The choice to withhold God and His love leads to a broken fellowship with God. "Abiding in Him" becomes impossible. There is a disconnection from the desires and power of God.

ANGER   RESENTMENT

HURT   SADNESS

DISAPPOINTMENT

FEAR   INSECURITIES

WOUNDEDNESS

Negative Emotions

How to Replace Negative Emotions with God's Love

1. Be honest with yourself and God. Are there any hurtful ways in me?
(Ps. 139:23–24)
- anger—Ephesians 4:26–31
- hurt—Colossians 3:13; Matt. 18:21–34
- fear—Philippians 4:6–7; 1 Peter 5:7

Have any of these feelings led you toward hurtful ways?

2. Confess and repent. Receive God's forgiveness, and be restored in your fellowship with Him (Rev. 2:4–5; 1 John 1:9).

3. Ask God to give you a clean heart and to fill it with His love (Ps. 51:10).

4. Now you can "abide in Him" and release His love (1 John 4:16).

AGAPE LOVE

FORGIVENESS

FRUIT OF THE SPIRIT
("Love, joy, peace. . . . ")

A Clean Heart

FORGIVENESS: KEY TO RESTORING RELATIONSHIPS

Student Worksheet for Chapter 4

The resistance to forgive is humanly instinctive. It's understandable. Our sense of justice concludes that the hurtful person doesn't deserve forgiveness. Especially, if that person doesn't even recognize their wrongdoing.

Our forgiveness was not deserved either. We desperately needed God's forgiveness and are so glad we have received it! Since God commanded that we forgive, the issue of forgiving is more about our relationship with God, than it is with the other person.

The decision to *not* forgive, is a choice to not obey God. This is willful sin. Share what these verses say about sin and forgiveness.

1. Isaiah 59:2; 1 John:6–7 _____

_____

2. 1 John 1:9 _____

_____

3. Matthew 18:23–35; Ephesians 4:32; Colossians 3:13 _____

_____

4. Luke 23:34_____

_____

You don't need the other person's cooperation. Sometimes, they are already dead or unavailable. Forgiving brings inner healing to the forgiver and insures a right relationship with God.

5. Romans 12:17–19 _____

_____

6. Matthew 18:21–22 _____

_____

7. Matthew 5:23–24; 18:15; Romans 12:18 _____

_____

_____

It is always your turn. God just wants to get it accomplished. It is too important to God, to be waiting on the other. In many cases, reconciliation would never happen otherwise.

8. 2 Corinthians 2:10–11 _____

_____

Forgiving from the Heart

1. Decide to forgive in obedience to the Lord. Leave the justice to God. Forgiveness is working on resolving your pain and leaving the other person to God.

2. Set aside one to two hours for unhurried time alone with God. Ask God to reveal all those who have hurt or offended you. Make a list of names.

3. Let God search the depths of your heart. To forgive from the heart, you must face the hurt, anger, bitterness, or hatred.

4. Take the list of names. Pray aloud for each person on the list. Take your time. "Lord God, I forgive (name) for (whatever has hurt or angered you), which made me feel (feelings). I choose to forgive (name), and I leave him/her in your hands. Amen."

5. Destroy the list. Thank God for your inner freedom. Your forgiveness is between you and God. There is no need to tell the other persons, unless they have asked you for forgiveness.

6. The healing will take time. The time will come when you will be able to think of them without feeling hurt or anger.

CONFLICT IN THE CHURCH

Student Worksheet for Chapter 5

The church in conflict has lost its spiritual focus. Many begin to engage in actions to save the church from those they blame for the problems. There is disunity of spirit and damaged relationships. There is distrust and disrespect for the leadership.

The congregation must return to the Biblical foundations for church life.

State a principle from each of the Scriptural foundations.

1. Colossians 1:18 _____

_____

2. 1 Corinthians 12:14–27 _____

_____

3. Ephesians 5:25 _____

_____

4. Colossians 1:22 _____

_____

5. John 17:20–23, 26 _____

_____

_____

6. Matthew 18:15–17 _____

_____

7. Ephesians 4:1–4, 15–16, 25–32; Colossians 3:12–15; 1 Corinthians 1:10

_____

_____

8. Matthew 5:23–24; 2 Corinthians 5:18 _____

_____

9. 1 John 1:6–9; 2 Chronicles 7:14

_____

_____

_____

BIBLICAL CONFLICT RESOLUTION

Student Worksheet for Chapter 6

Jesus gave clear step-by-step instructions on how to righteously resolve conflicts among Christians. His instructions can be found in Matthew 5:23–24; 18:15–17. When this biblical procedure is followed with a redemptive and loving spirit, He confers heavenly authority on the decision of the church, and promises His powerful presence (Matt. 18:18–20).

1. If you have offended someone, you should _____ _____(Matt. 5:23–24).

2. _____ is foremost on God's priority list (Matt. 5:23–24; 2 Cor. 5:18). Reconciliation is the core message of the Bible, man with God and with each other.

Before going to confront someone, consider the following principles.

a. Examine yourself before God (Ps. 139:23–24).
Do I have any unconfessed sin? Have I offended him? Have I failed to be a Christlike example? Have I considered how I can help him overcome the problem?

b. Scrutinize your wording to be non-offensive.
"I have decided that I will only share positive information about you to anyone who asks. For this reason I wonder if you could help me explain something I am not sure I understand."
"Have I done something wrong to cause you to react in this way?"
" I have had a problem in the past with this area. . . . "

c. Search out your resistance to going to him and confronting him in private.

•Your own sins prevent you.
•You have already told it to others.
•Your pride prevents you from revealing that he was able to hurt you.
•Procrastination.
•Doubt. You don't believe it will do any good. You tried it before. (Warning: Don't exalt your experience over the Lord's command.)
•Ignorance. Now you are no longer ignorant of Jesus' instruction.

d. Check your motive. Commit yourself to only giving a good report of others, unless you have followed the steps of Matthew 18, and in the right spirit.

3. If someone has offended you, you should _____ _____. This should be done in private to guard his dignity, treating him with the respect and value that God extends to all His children. The goal is to _____, not hurt him (Matt.18:15). The test of spirituality is not to expose sin, but to restore the sinner.

4. It is at this juncture that most Christians falter. Instead of talking secretly _____the offendee talks secretly to others _____ _____

This is sin! It is a sin against God's Word and against your brother. God hates gossip. However, the devil loves gossip because it is through this channel that he spreads ill feelings, distortions, and discord. Gossip in the church is so prevalent that I felt a strong need to provide a separate study on this destructive sin in the church (★See Appendix K).

If you are not directly the offended one, the Bible gives instruction to become involved to help the brother who has fallen (Gal.6:1).

5. If the sinner does not repent, then Jesus gives instruction to widen the appeal to a _____

_____(Matt. 18:16).

The witnesses can be verifiers of the truth about the allegation(s), or serve as witnesses to whether he repents or not.

The meeting is to be confidential. If the sinner repents, but others have already heard about his sins, his reputation is unfairly and unnecessarily hurt. "Therefore whatever you want others to do for you, do so for them" (Matt. 7:12). The reputation of the repentant sinner is not to be previously maligned.

6. If after meeting with a small group, there is still no repentance or resolution, then the matter must be brought forward for the church to resolve. Hopefully, this public scrutiny will motivate repentance. If not, church discipline must follow. Most churches disobey Christ and don't carry out this final step. Chapter seven provides guidelines for carrying out church discipline. Church discipline should be done with a redemptive spirit, and only as a last measure.

BIBLICAL BASIS FOR CHURCH DISCIPLINE

Student Worksheet for Chapter 7

Why should the church be diligent to carry out church discipline?

_____

_____

(Matt. 18:17; 1 Cor. 5:1–13; Titus 3:10; Rom. 16:17)

Church discipline should be exercised . . .
1. 1 Corinthians 5:1–13 _____

_____

_____

2. 1 Timothy 5:20 _____

_____

_____

3. Titus 1:10–11 _____

_____

_____

4. Galatians 6:1; Hebrews 12:10–13; James 5:20; 2 Thessalonians 3:14–15

_____

_____

_____

5. 2 Samuel 12:14; 1 Peter 1:14; 2:9

_____

_____

6. Acts 20:28; Galatians 5:16 _____

_____

_____

7. Titus 1:13 _____

_____

_____

8. Hebrews 12:10–13 _____

_____

_____

CONGREGATIONAL QUESTIONNAIRE

How long have you attended the church?_____
or How long has it been since you have attended the church?_____
Do you serve in any position in the church? Yes____ No____
If yes, please indicate:_____

1. What are some of the strengths of this church?

2. What are some of the weaknesses?

3. Are you aware of any unresolved conflicts or unreconciled relationships? If so, please identify them.

4. What concerns do you have about the future of the church?

5. What suggestions for future actions do you feel are necessary?

6. What one goal or dream do you personally have for the church?

Name_____ **Phone**_____

CONFLICT RESOLUTION SESSION BRIEFING

Preparation Briefing Sheet

The purpose of this meeting is to gain reconciliation in your relationship with the one who has offended you. This is God's will for every broken or strained relationship.

This is a bold step of obedience in the conflict resolution procedure that Jesus clearly outlined. "And if your brother sins, go and reprove him in private; if he listens you have won your brother. But if he does not listen to you, take one or two more with you, so that by the mouth of two or three witnesses every fact may be confirmed" (Matt. 18:15–16).

The presence of non-biased witnesses is used by God to facilitate a peaceful and productive process of resolving conflicts. Our prayer is that the relationship will be reconciled for the honor and glory of God. The Bible says that we are to be ministers of reconciliation (2 Cor. 5:18).

This process is intended to only deal with serious offenses, where the unrepentant offender may require church discipline. On one or more issues, there may be no further step beyond agreeing to disagree. In order to have satisfactory resolution, avoid presenting opinions but present facts with evidence, Scriptural support and witnesses, if possible. Unless the offense is verifiable, the witnesses cannot confirm the facts.

Please prayerfully review the following Biblical guidelines. Read each of the Scriptural passages.

1. Speak the truth in love. Avoid sarcasm (Eph. 4:15).
2. Approach with a spirit of gentleness (Gal. 6:1).
3. Avoid derogatory statements that attack one's character (Eph. 4:29).
4. Seek the unity of the Spirit (Eph. 4:1–3).
5. Be willing to forgive and reconcile (Eph. 4:32).

SAMPLE REPORT OF CHURCH EVALUATIONS AND RECOMMENDATIONS

First Baptist Church

First Baptist Church has experienced a very serious crisis in the past months. The church has been struggling with a major budget deficit. This deficit was the result of two financial decisions that the church made earlier in the year. The church voted to raise the pastor's salary and purchase some property.

Those decisions added a significant amount to the fixed budget expenditures. Evidently, there hadn't been a stewardship program to promote the increase in giving to underwrite the adjusted budget. The congregation has had four business meetings to make various decisions to balance the budget.

During this financial problem solving, a deeper spiritual problem has emerged. Evidently, there were unresolved issues from the past that have created tension, frustration, and even hostility among some of the leadership.

Some have been deeply offended and hurt, thus causing a major rift in the fellowship. At times, chaos and verbal wars have occurred. The church has incurred a "black eye" and the witness of the gospel hindered. The messages of love, peace, unity, brotherhood, forgiveness, and reconciliation are drowned in the noise of hurtful church fighting.

The need for individual and corporate repentance is unmistakable and imperative. "And if my people who are called by My name humble themselves and pray, and seek My face and turn from their wicked ways, then I will hear from heaven, will forgive their sin, and will heal their land" (2 Chron. 7:14).

After meeting with the church leadership, I observed a willing spirit to take corporate responsibility for the church problems, and not blame any individuals. There were references to actions taken that were not brought before the church and violated the church constitution. However, it was recognized that those actions were allowed by the church by not exercising congregational authority to the contrary. This is how unwarranted authority is countered in a Baptist church.

It was also acknowledged that in the past, the congregation had not been fully informed on different issues. Whenever there is a lack of public knowledge, there is danger for misunderstandings and wrong perceptions because of distorted facts from rumors.

The church leadership affirmed the privilege of members to be informed, but also admonished each other about the responsibility of involvement and commitment. There appears to be a resolve to take responsibility for future church life, for the glory of God. Some expressed a hopeful outlook.

My evaluation and recommendations have resulted from information provided from a consultation with [the pastor?], including his gleanings from the two listening sessions, church documents, pastoral interviews, and the meeting with the church leaders. In assessing this information, the conflicts can be resolved and the prevention of future similar problems, by actions taken in the following areas:

    I. Interpersonal Conflicts
    II. Church Administration Guidelines
    III. Church Polity and Constitution

The recommendations include actions that could bring spiritual healing and renewal. The congregation would be able to proceed forward and refocus on the church's mission, with a more efficient church management system.

Your Church Covenant is recorded in the Church Constitution. If you fulfill this covenant, the future of the church will be God-honoring, will bless the people of God, and make an eternal difference in your community.

Church Covenant

"Having been led, as we believe, by the spirit of God, to receive the Lord Jesus Christ as our Savior, and on the profession of our faith, having been baptized in the name of the Father, and of the Son, and of the Holy Spirit we do now in the presence of God and this assembly, most solemnly and joyfully enter into covenant with one another, as one body in Christ.

We engage, therefore, by the aid of the Holy Spirit, to walk together in Christian love; to strive for the advancement of this church in knowledge, holiness, and comfort; to promote its prosperity and spirituality; to sustain its worship, ordinances, discipline, and doctrine; to contribute cheerfully and regularly to the support of the ministry, the expenses of the church, the relief of the poor and the spread of the Gospel through all nations.

We also engage to maintain family and secret devotions; to teach our children the Christian truths; to seek the salvation of our kindred and acquaintances; to walk circum-spectly in the world; to avoid all tattling, and backbiting and excessive anger; to abstain from the sale and use of intoxicating drink as a beverage, and be zealous in our efforts to advance the Kingdom of our Savior.

We further engage to watch over one another with brotherly love; to remember each other in prayer; to aid each other in sickness or distress; to cultivate Christian sympathy in feeling and courtesy of speech; to be slow to take offense but always ready for reconciliation, and mindful of the teachings of our Savior to secure it without delay.

We moreover engage that when we move from this area, we will as soon as possible unite with some other church where we can carry on the spirit of this covenant and the principles of God's Word."

I. INTERPERSONAL CONFLICTS

A. DEFINITION OF THE PROBLEM

1. There were two hostile instances on the first weekend of September that still draw a strong emotional reaction. The first situation was a finance committee/trustees meeting. The second was the Sunday morning service. Those two occasions seemed to be very offensive to many present. There also seem to be strained or broken relationships from past incidences.

B. RECOMMENDATIONS

1. Every member needs to focus on self and examine under God's guidance, whether there is any personal fault that needs acknowledgment to God. The following scriptural path is suggested:

Psalm 139:23–24

Psalm 51:1–4; 10–13, 17

1 John 1:8–9

2. If there is someone that one has offended or sinned against, reconciliatory actions should be taken. The following Biblical guidelines should be followed:

Matthew 5:23–24

James 5:16

3. If someone has been sinned against, the Lord instructs the offendee to approach the offender. Confront the offender privately and if necessary, with witnesses, to restore relationship (Matt. 18:15–16). If the offendee is unwilling to confront, then the offendee must be willing to forgive. The following scriptures clearly mandate the Christian to fulfill the standard of forgiveness. An unforgiving spirit is never justified (Matt. 18:21–35; Eph. 4:32).

4. Plan a Spiritual Renewal Weekend event that will focus on the Lordship of Christ. The intent would be to refocus on the Lord's headship of His church, His will and the church's mission. This event should also include teaching on how to restore relationships and gain healing.

C. IMPLEMENTATION: Schedule this weekend by the church council, invite an outside facilitator to lead this critical event.

II. CHURCH ADMINISTRATION

A. DEFINITION OF THE PROBLEM

The church encountered a financial crisis because of the impact of two decisions, purchase of property and an increase of the pastor's salary. The monthly church income could not sustain the budget increases from those added monthly expenditures.

The budget shortage created the predicament of not being able to pay all the monthly debts or obligations. The lack of paying budgeted mission commitments were met with congregational disfavor.

B. RECOMMENDATIONS

1. The Church Constitution and Bylaws need to be amended. It should include more specific instructions to the treasurer for a priority payment policy, whenever

there is a lack of monies to pay all of the church budget's obligations. (This is an unfair responsibility to place on an individual or committee).

2. There should be an ongoing stewardship emphasis, keeping the congregation challenged to support the church budget.

3. Provide monthly reports to the members to keep them updated on budget needs.

C. IMPLEMENTATION: The stewardship committee should bring a recommendation for a priority payment policy when there are insufficient funds. The congregation should approve a priority payment policy to be included in the Church Constitution under "Officers; Section 3, Treasurer." The stewardship Committee can contact Rod Wiltrout, CSBC, for consultation on plans for stewardship emphasis.

III. CHURCH POLICY

A. DEFINITION OF THE PROBLEM

The church Constitution does not contain any information about church committees. There must be clarity about the responsibility and duties, meeting and reporting regularity.

There is a lack of guidelines for the conducting of church business, including the regularity of business meetings and the calling of special business meetings.

B. RECOMMENDATION

An ad hoc Constitution Revision Committee be elected for the purpose of recommending necessary amendments or complete constitutional revision.

C. IMPLEMENTATION: The Nominating Committee should recommend persons for church approval, to form the Constitution Revision Committee. Secure sample descriptions of other church constitutions, church committee descriptions and governing bylaws. These can be secured from Greg Sumii, CSBC.

THE DESTRUCTIVE SIN OF GOSSIP

Gossip is a sin against God. God clearly condemns gossip in the Bible. Gossip is also a sin against the person who is the subject of the gossip. It is a malicious action that hurts his reputation. It is clearly gossip when the person talked about is not included. There is no possible remedy without the person present to clarify, refute, or resolve the issue causing concern.

Gossip is a sin against a third party, the person with whom it is shared. It places an unfair burden on that person. It also contaminates the relationship and impression with the person who is the object of the gossip.

The person who listens to the gossiper is also guilty of sin. Without a conduit, gossip cannot be spread. By listening to the gossiper, one passively encourages the sinful activity.

Gossip is sometimes presented in a pretentious righteous context. It is said, "We need to be in prayer for Brother Joe, because . . . (the gossip)." The oddity is that they never seem to get around to praying together for that person!

1. How serious is the sin of gossip, anyway? (Rom. 1:28–32)

_____

_____

2. How should we react to gossip and other sins in the fellowship? (2 Cor. 12:20–21; Prov. 20:19; 2 Tim. 3:5)

_____

_____

3. How can we proactively stop gossipers? (Matt. 18:15–17; Eph. 5:11)

_____

_____

A gossiper in the church is poisonous to the fellowship. Gossip is the devil's scheming medium to spread mistrust, disrespect, deception, slander and discord. His goal is to cause division and strife, distract the church from its mission, and eventually disgrace the witness of Christ and His great love.

It is every Christian's responsibility to stop gossip by refusing to listen to it. Ask the gossiper if they have followed Jesus' guidelines in Matthew 18:15–17. For the honor and glory of God, stop the gossip!

RECOMMENDED RESOURCES

Chapter 1

The Adversary, Mark I. Bubeck, Moody Press, 1975.

Overcoming The Adversary, Mark I. Bubeck, Moody Press, 1984.

The Bondage Breaker, Neil T. Anderson, Regal Books, 1990.

Chapter 2

The Anger Workbook, Carter/Minirth, Thomas Nelson, Inc., 1993.

Overcoming Hurts and Anger, Dwight L. Carlson, Harvest House Publishers, 1981.

Chapter 3

Love, Acceptance, and Forgiveness, Cook/Baldwin, Regal Books, 1979.

What You Feel You Can Heal, John Gray, Heart Publishing, 1984.

Men Are From Mars, Women Are From Venus, John Gray, Heart Publishing, 1992.

Heart Connections, Gordon and Gail Macdonald, Revell, 1997.

Chapter 4

The Art of Forgiving, Lewis B. Smedes, Moorings, 1996.

Forgive and Forget, Lewis B. Smedes, Simon and Schuster, Inc., 1984.

The Freedom of Forgiveness, David Augsburger, Moody Press, 1988.

Chapter 5

Well-Intentioned Dragons, Marshall Shelley, Christianity Today, Inc., 1985.

Church Conflict, Charles H. Cosgrove, Abington Press, 1989.

Chapter 6

Resolving Conflict in the Church, Pastor to Pastor Tape Series, Focus On the Family, 1993.

Win-Win Relationships, H. Newton Malony, Broadman and Holman, 1995.

Managing Church Conflict, Hugh F. Halverstadt, Westminster/John Knox Press, 1991.

The Peacemaker, Ken Sande, Baker Book House, 1991.

Chapter 7

A Guide to Church Discipline, J. Carl Laney, Bethany House Publishers, 1985.

Handbook of Church Discipline, Jay Adams, Zondervan Publishing House, 1988.

Chapter 8

Sanctify the Congregation, Richard Owen Roberts, International Awakening Press, 1994.

Fresh Encounter, Henry T. Blackaby and Claude King, Lifeway Press, 1993.

The Power of Prayer and Fasting, Ronnie W. Floyd, Broadman and Holman, 1997.